The Soil

By Shannon David
Illustrated by Yuwak Shrestha

Library For All Ltd.

Library For All is an Australian not for profit organisation with a mission to make knowledge accessible to all via an innovative digital library solution. Visit us at libraryforall.org

The Soil

This edition published 2022

Published by Library For All Ltd
Email: info@libraryforall.org
URL: libraryforall.org

Library For All gratefully acknowledges the contributions of all who made previous editions of this book possible.

Room to Read®

www.roomtoread.org

Original illustrations by Yuwak Shrestha

The Soil
David, Shannon
ISBN: 978-1-922918-96-3
SKU03044

The Soil

Look at the soil, my friend. The grass is so green here!

This is where flowers bloom. They smell so sweet!

This is where rice and wheat grow.

This is where the
potatoes and sweet
potatoes grow!

The soil is where the mud dauber builds its nest.

A mud dauber is a type of wasp that makes nests out of mud, which is wet soil.

The swallow makes her nest out of soil too! She carries it in her beak.

This soil is where the crocodile lays her eggs.

And that soil is where
the chameleon gives
births to her young.

Look, my friend. This
soil is where the horses
and the elephants live!

This is where the
days break.

This is where we play and dance. The soil is our life!

You can use these questions to talk about this book with your family, friends and teachers.

What did you learn from this book?

Describe this book in one word.
Funny? Scary? Colourful? Interesting?

How did this book make you feel when you finished reading it?

What was your favourite part of this book?

download our reader app
getlibraryforall.org

About the contributors

Library For All works with authors and illustrators from around the world to develop diverse, relevant, high quality stories for young readers. Visit libraryforall.org for the latest news on writers' workshop events, submission guidelines and other creative opportunities.

Did you enjoy this book?

We have hundreds more expertly curated original stories to choose from.

We work in partnership with authors, educators, cultural advisors, governments and NGOs to bring the joy of reading to children everywhere.

Did you know?

We create global impact in these fields by embracing the United Nations Sustainable Development Goals.

libraryforall.org

www.ingramcontent.com/pod-product-compliance
Lightning Source LLC
Chambersburg PA
CBHW040317050426
42452CB00018B/2879